Steve Jobs:
the man behind Apple

Rod Smith

Richmond READERS

Richmond READERS

LEVEL 1

(500 headwords)

Maria's Dilemma

Oscar

Jack's Game

The Boy from Yesterday

The Black Mountain

LEVEL 2

(800 headwords)

Jason Causes Chaos

Craigen Castle Mystery

The Road through the Hills and othes stories

Where's Mauriac?

Saturday Storm

LEVEL 3

(1200 headwords)

A Trip to the Stars

Dr Jekyll and Mr Hyde

The Canterville Ghost and Other Stories

Cold Feet

Frankenstein

LEVEL 4

(1800 headwords)

A Trip to London

Dracula

Jane Eyre

The Adventures of Tom Sawyer

Sense and Sensibility

LEVEL 5

(2600+ headwords)

Steve Jobs: the man behind Apple

Elizabeth II The Diamond Queen

Contents

People in the Story

Steve and his friend Steve Wozniak, known as 'Woz', met at a computer club at Homestead High School in 1970. They became good friends and formed the Apple Computer Company in 1976. Their first product was called the Apple I computer.

Laurene Powell is Steve Job's wife. They met in October, 1989, and were married two years later. They had three children: two girls - Erin and Eve, and a boy - Reed.

Bill Gates formed the Microsoft Company in 1976. Since then, it has been the world's main provider of computer operating software. Microsoft and Apple have been rivals* for many years but Bill and Steve respected each other. On hearing of Steve's death, Bill said: "I am truly saddened … I will miss Steve greatly."

John Sculley joined Apple from the Pepsi Cola Company in 1983. At first, he and Steve Jobs were friends but they soon disagreed about how to make Apple more successful. After John Scully became president of Apple, Steve left the company and Apple's sales began to fall. Steve later said that Sculley was "destroying Apple."

Mona Simpson is Steve Job's sister. She is a well-known author and professor of English at the University of California. They met in 1985, after Steve went to look for his real family. They were very close friends for the rest of Steve's life.

Jony Ive is an English designer who is the head of Apple's design team. In 1997, he wanted to leave the company because he thought Apple were more interested in making money than designing good products. When Steve returned to Apple, he persuaded Jony to stay. Jony agreed. He went on to design the iPod, iPad, iPhone and many of Apple's best products.

Introduction

Steve Jobs was the greatest business leader of modern times. When he left Apple, the company he formed with Steve Wozniak, in 1985, its market share* in computer products was 15%. By 1997, the year Steve returned to Apple, this had fallen to 3.8% and Time magazine were describing it as 'a company with no future'.

They were wrong. Apple's market share now stands at over 23%. But numbers don't tell the whole story. Apart from its commercial success, Apple is now the most creative and admired company in the world. One man, more than any other, was responsible for Apple's rise from failure to success. His name was Steve Jobs.

This is his story.

The Boy With No Name

"Mama don't go, Daddy come home"
(From the song: 'Mother' by John Lennon)

When Joanne Scheible and her boyfriend, Abdulfattah Jandali, went to Syria to visit his parents in the summer of 1954, they didn't plan on having a child. But on their return to the United States, Joanne found out that she was pregnant*. The news came as a shock. Joanne was a student at the University of Wisconsin. Abdulfattah, although only twenty-three years old, was one of her teachers. They wanted to get married, but Joanne's father said no. He was dying at the time and told Joanne that he would leave her with no money if she married Abdulfattah. The couple agreed not to get married and Joanne went to San Francisco to have the baby, alone.

On February 24th, 1955, Joanne Scheible gave birth to a baby boy. He wasn't given a name. Joanne and Abdulfattah simply called him 'the boy' and decided to have him adopted*. For Joanne, there was one important condition. Whoever took her son had to agree to give him a university education when he was old enough.

The enquiry about adopting their son, came from a professional couple who could afford to pay for a university education. But at the last minute they changed their minds and decided they wanted a girl instead.

The next couple seemed less suitable. Their names were

Paul and Clara Jobs. Paul was a mechanic*, Clara was an office worker who was unable to have children of her own for medical reasons. They were rather poor and not very well educated. Despite this, they promised to give Joanne's son a university education when the time came. At first Joanne said no, but when she saw how kind and hard-working they were she agreed to let them take her son.

The first thing Paul and Clara did was to give their new son a name. They called him Steven Paul Jobs. For the rest of his life, Steve always thought of Paul and Clara as his real parents and never entirely forgave Joanne and Abdulfattah for abandoning him.

Paul and Clara were very honest with Steve about his adoption.

'We looked at a lot of children,' they told him. 'And we chose you.'

These opposite feelings of being both 'abandoned' and 'specially chosen' would have a strong effect on the development of Steve's personality.

• • •

When Steve was two, the family moved to Mountain View, a small town just south of San Francisco. Paul loved machines and even before Steve started school he was showing him how they worked. Soon they were building their own and spent hours in the family garage making anything from wooden cars to paper aeroplanes. Steve was very interested in how they worked and learnt quickly.

The same was not true at his first school, Monta Loma Elementary, which he started at the age of five. He was bored by school subjects and spent most of his time playing tricks on the teachers. Sometimes he was sent home. But his father blamed the school, not his son. "It's your fault if you can't keep him interested," he said.

When he was nine, Steve eventually met a teacher he liked. Her name was Teddy Hill. Steve did so well with Teddy that the school decided to put him in grade* six a year early. Monta Loma's highest grade was five. This meant Steve had to change schools. His new school was called Crittenden Middle School.

Crittenden was a disaster. Because Steve was younger and generally cleverer than the other children, they treated him badly. Steve hated the school. Every day, he thought about one thing above all else: going home. At home he was safe. At home he could work with his father in the family garage. They were now building radios and other electronic machines. Already, Steve had a better understanding of electronics than his father.

At the end of Steve's second year at Crittenden things were so bad that he told his parents, 'If I have to go back to Crittenden, I'll stop going to school altogether.'

His parents knew they had to do something. They began looking for a better school. The nearest was in Los Altos. This was a more expensive area but Paul and Clara put together all the money they had and bought a house there.

Steve's new school was called Homestead High. It was close to Silicon Valley, the centre of America's growing technology industry. Because of this, science and technology were important subjects at the school. Steve made friends with a group of older students who were interested in electronics. They introduced him to the Explorer's Club. This was held in the cafeteria of the

Hewlett Packard factory, not far from the school. The club's members were encouraged to design their own electronics projects*. Steve built a loudspeaker system in his house. It was controlled from his bedroom and allowed him to listen to what was happening in any of the other rooms. When his father found out, Steve had to take it away.

Steve also got a summer job in the Hewlett Packard factory. By the time he was fifteen, he had saved up enough money to buy his own car. It was only an old car, but he and his father managed to get it in good working condition.

Interesting things were happening at school, too. A new electronics class had opened. The teacher was John McCollum. He was a good teacher but Steve thought he had too much respect for authority. Steve had almost no respect for authority and this annoyed McCollum.

"Steve was always doing things without permission," McCollum said.

In the end, Steve took the class for only one year out of the three that were offered. But before he left, he formed one of the most important friendships of his life. His new friend was a graduate student who was five years older than him. He taught the students in McCollum's class. His name was Steve Wozniak but everyone called him 'Woz'.

CHAPTER 2

'Woz'

CD1

"I was too shy ever to be a business leader."
(Steve Wozniak)

Like Steve, Woz learned a lot from his father. But they were quite different. Paul Jobs was a practical man who understood mechanics and enjoyed building things. Francis Wozniak was an important electronics engineer at the Lockheed Aerospace Company. To Francis, engineering was more than just a job. He believed it was the most important thing anyone could do in life. He communicated this enthusiasm to his son. From an early age, Woz learnt to value engineering above all else. His father was a great teacher, too, and made the subject extremely interesting. One of Woz's earliest memories was playing with electronic parts his father had put on a table for him to look at. By fourth grade, almost the only things Woz read were his father's weekly electronics magazines. He had also learnt how to design and build a variety of complicated machines. One of these was an advanced scientific calculator, which won the top prize in a local competition.

Two other things Francis taught Woz would stay with him for the rest of his life. The first was honesty.

"Never lie," his father said.

Woz listened. He became known as someone who either told the truth or said nothing.

The second thing his father taught him was the danger of extreme ambition.

"Don't head for the top," Francis told Woz. "There's too much stress. Just be happy in the middle, doing what you're good at."

This suited Woz. He was shy and didn't enjoy being the centre of attention.

In this sense, he was very different from Steve. Steve was ambitious. He liked to lead and was very good at directing other people.

In other ways, they were similar. Apart from their enthusiasm for electronics, they had a similar sense of humour and shared a love for the same kind of music.

Their musical heroes were Bob Dylan and the Beatles. Steve and Woz would often stay up late at night reading the words of Dylan's songs and trying to understand what they meant.

Their shared sense of humour often got them into trouble. The most famous occasion was at a formal school event one summer. Steve and Woz had built a machine which lowered a rude sign painted on a white sheet. They turned it on at the most serious part of the event. The other students laughed but the teachers were not amused. They couldn't do anything to Woz because he'd already left school, but Steve was sent home for a week.

• • •

In Steve's last year at Homestead High, he and Woz began an adventure that started as a joke and ended as a business. Many years later, Steve said that it led to the creation of Apple. There was only one problem. It was illegal.

Woz got the idea from a report he read in one of his mother's magazines. It was about a young man called John Draper. Draper had discovered that a free whistle from a packet of breakfast food produced the same sound as one of the telephone signals used for long distance calls. By blowing the whistle into the telephone he was able to make calls for free. Woz thought he could build a machine which would produce all the sounds the telephone company used. If he was successful, all calls, including long distance ones, could be made for free.

He called Steve and told him of his idea. Steve was very excited. He knew Woz could make it work. They managed to find a technical telephone book that described all the electronic sounds they needed. Woz couldn't build the machine immediately because he was about to start a course at Berkeley College, but he promised to build it once he was there.

Woz kept his promise. A short time later, he called Steve and told him that the machine was ready. They decided to call it 'The Blue Box' and agreed to test it later the same day.

Woz drove over to Steve's house and they used the blue box to call his uncle in Los Angeles. They got through to Los Angeles but it was the wrong number. That didn't matter. The important thing was that the device* had worked. They had made a long distance call for free.

Steve immediately saw the commercial possibilities. The parts for one blue box cost $40. He thought they could sell them for $150. It was a good size, too, and could easily fit inside a jacket pocket. Woz's electronics might have been complicated but the blue box was easy to use. It was the first example of a product whose success was helped by Woz and Steve's different roles. Woz was the technical genius*, Steve saw how to direct this genius into making things people wanted and could use easily. Their roles

were different, but helpful to each other. Later, these would prove very important in making Apple a successful company.

But this was still some years away. For now, Steve and Woz were happy just to make a little money by tricking the telephone system.

They started producing blue boxes late in 1971. At nights during the week and at weekends they took them to accommodation buildings in colleges and demonstrated how they worked. They were immediately popular with students who loved the idea of beating the telephone system.

The blue boxes sold well enough to worry the

telephone company. They realised that someone had discovered their technical sound information and began removing all their technical books from local libraries.

Two things ended Woz and Steve's blue box adventure. The first happened in a pizza restaurant. One day, after ordering a pizza, the two friends were sitting playing with one of their blue boxes. A group of young men at the next table seemed interested in the device. Steve offered to demonstrate how it worked in a telephone box outside the restaurant. After the demonstration, the leader of the group told Steve he wanted to buy it but that the money was in his car. Steve gave him the device and they walked over to his vehicle. When they arrived, the man opened the door, reached inside, then turned around with a gun in his hand. Steve told him to keep the blue box and walked away.

The other problem was that Steve and Woz were breaking the law. They had been able to ignore this for a while but the police were becoming more involved. Neither of them wanted to get caught, so they gave up producing and selling their devices.

After this, Woz went back to his studies at Berkeley and Steve, now in his final year at high school, began to think of university.

It would soon be time for Paul and Clara to keep their promise to Joanne Scheible.

As usual, Steve wouldn't make it easy.

Love and Spiritualism

"Steve was kind of crazy. That's why I was attracted to him." (Chrisann Brennan)

With the blue box adventure behind him, Steve turned to his other interests. One of these was literature. He especially enjoyed reading the works of Shakespeare and Plato. His favourite Shakespeare play was King Lear. Eastern spiritualism, particularly Buddhism*, was another interest. It led to an obsession* for strange diets which would last throughout his life. For weeks at a time, Steve would eat nothing but fruits and vegetables. This made him very thin.

Many students at the school thought Steve was rather a strange person. This was something he encouraged because he enjoyed being seen as different to everyone else. He even took the trouble to develop this difference. One of the ways he did this was by learning to stare at people without ever blinking. Some felt uncomfortable. Others were attracted by it. One of these was a girl called Chrisann Brennan. She was a pretty girl with light brown hair and green eyes who was having a difficult time at home because her parents were getting divorced. She was attracted to Steve because she sensed an emotional pain inside him similar to her own. After working together in class on a short, animated* movie, they began dating. Within a few weeks she had become his first serious girlfriend.

• • •

Steve had also begun experimenting with drugs. His first serious argument at home happened over drugs. One day, his father discovered some drugs in Steve's car. He told him to promise never to take them again. Steve refused. After this, they didn't speak to each other for days.

Steve's second serious argument with his father was over his plans with Chrisann.

He came home from school one day and announced, "Chrisann and I are going to live together for the summer in a place up in the hills."

"No, you're not," his father replied.

It made no difference. After a short argument, Steve left home.

At first, Steve and Chrisann's time living together was wonderful. They shared the same opinion on most things and had similar artistic interests. Chrisann loved to paint, while Steve enjoyed playing guitar and writing poetry. But it wasn't all peace and love. Sometimes Steve could be rude and cruel. "There was this big darkness around him," Chrisann said later.

The bad feeling between Steve and his father ended after only a few weeks. One day, he was driving along the highway in his old car, when the engine caught fire. He pulled the car off the road, jumped out, ran to a telephone box and called home. Paul came immediately to take him back to Los Altos. It was near the end of summer so Chrisann also returned home.

The most important subject Steve's family needed to discuss was the question of his college education. He could have joined Woz at Berkeley College. Stanford was also a possibility. It had the advantage of being nearby. But Steve wouldn't consider either of these. He had been accepted at a place called Reed College. It was a famous, but very expensive, private college in Oregon. His parents tried to make him change his mind.

"If you can't afford it I don't have to go to college at all," Steve told them.

This was out of the question. Paul and Clara had made a promise and they meant to keep it. They put all their money together. There was just enough to pay for Steve's first year.

• • •

Steve arrived at Reed College in the autumn of 1972. It was a small college with only one thousand students. A lot of them had chosen to go there because, like Steve, they had been rebels* in the formal school system and were attracted by Reed's free, open environment.

This freedom, however, was rather shallow. Beneath its informality, Reed College was very serious about its educational standards. Students had to work hard and follow exactly the subjects they had chosen.

By the end of his first week at Reed, Steve had made friends with another student called Dan Kottke. He and Steve shared many of the same interests. They liked the same music, were interested in Buddhism, and enjoyed taking drugs. Dan came from a wealthy New York family but his interest in Buddhism had turned him against wanting to have material things.

For Steve, Dan, and Dan's girlfriend, Elizabeth Holmes, Buddhism became a passion. The biggest influence it had on Steve was the importance it gave to intuition*, or trusting what you feel. This was far more important to Steve than getting knowledge from other people, no matter how respected they were.

He was also influenced by the value Buddhism gave to leading a simple life, free of possessions. From that time on, the power of intuition and the beauty of simplicity would become the two guiding principles of Steve's life.

Steve's love of Buddhism made him lose interest in his studies. He couldn't see the point of the course he was taking. It didn't have any relation to what he wanted to do in life. After six months, he decided to give up being a student at Reed so that his parents would no longer have to pay for his education. But first, he asked if he could go to only the classes that interested him, even if he couldn't pay. The college agreed, but he wouldn't be able to take any exams. This was fine with Steve. He began mixing classes, going from science to arts subjects whenever he felt like it. Calligraphy* was the subject he was most interested in and the study of letters written by hand would have a strong influence on his sense of beauty and design. For the first time, Steve was able to put himself between the fields of art and technology. Years later, the results of this would amaze the world.

• • •

Dan Kottke also introduced Steve to a man called Robert Friedland. Friedland owned an apple farm, called the All One Farm. Steve and Dan spent weekends there and Steve eventually managed a small area of the farm. This experience would stay with him and was the reason he would choose the name 'apple' for his future company.

However, he soon saw the negative side of living in a large, shared community. He had been sleeping in the kitchen one night and woke up to find people stealing each other's food from the refrigerator. As at Reed, 'freedom' was very shallow.

After Steve left the farm, he managed to survive on very little money. He and Dan would go to the local Buddhist Centre for free meals and Steve was paid for doing small jobs around Reed College.

• • •

Early in 1974, Steve finally decided he'd had enough of Reed College and returned home. He arrived in February, feeling guilty, and immediately went to look for work. He had seen a job advertisement in a local paper. Atari, the video game company, were hiring people.

Steve arrived at the company's offices wearing old clothes and without having had a shower. He was not very polite and told the receptionist he wouldn't leave until the company gave him a job. The receptionist didn't know whether to call the police or her boss. In the end, she chose her boss, Al Alcorn. Despite Steve's messy appearance and direct manner, Alcorn quite liked him. He put him to work with one of Atari's engineers.

The next day, the engineer complained that he couldn't work next to someone who was rude and smelled so bad. Alcorn went to Steve and told him he would have to work nights in future because he was upsetting the other employees. Steve agreed and began working on his own at night, trying to improve Atari's video games. Because he was interested in the job, he worked hard and was successful in making them better.

• • •

One of the reasons Steve wanted to make money quickly

was to pay for a trip to India with his friend Dan Kottke. Dan just wanted to visit the country but Steve was hoping to find a spiritual teacher that Robert Friedland had told him about. The man's name was Neem Karoli Baba. He lived in a village near the town of Nainital in northern India. The trip would be expensive. Luckily for Steve, Atari were having trouble with some of their machines in Germany and someone had to go over to Europe and fix the problem. Steve offered to go - he knew it would be cheaper to travel to India from Europe than the USA - and the company agreed. After the work was finished, Steve would leave the company and go on to India from there. He would meet Dan in New Delhi.

The trip to Germany was a success. The trip to India wasn't. In Germany, Steve fixed the problem, with the machines, but in India he discovered that Neem had died. There were other problems, too. He fell ill soon after he arrived in New Delhi. Then Dan had all his money stolen. Steve was kind. He paid for Dan's food and gave him $100 so that his friend would have some money on the flight back home.

Steve spent a total of seven months in India without finding a spiritual teacher he was happy with. He'd had enough and decided to return home. He took a flight from New Delhi and arrived back at Oakland airport. His parents were waiting for him but they didn't recognise him at first. He looked tired, dirty, dark-skinned and disappointed.

Later, Steve would find a spiritual teacher he could trust, much nearer to home. His name was Kobun Chino. But for now, his search was over.

• • •

Soon after Steve arrived home, he contacted Woz. Woz was working for the Hewlett Packard company and told Steve of all the exciting things that had been happening with technology since he'd been away. They decided to explore these new possibilities together.

It was a decision that would change the world.

CHAPTER 4

The Birth of Apple

CD1

"Apple Computer? - it doesn't quite make sense!"
(Mike Markkula)

When Steve returned home in 1975, a big change was happening in the way people viewed communication technology. Since the discovery of the microchip* in the late 1950s, many people saw it as a danger. Governments, through the use of computers, would have greater power to control people. They feared that, if this continued, we could soon be living in the kind of nightmare world described by George Orwell in his famous book, 1984. But now, many of the young people who were good at technology were also interested in making the world freer, rather than more controlled. A large number of these individuals were interested in music, art, and creative ways of thinking. If computers could be made smaller and more personal, they could act as a powerful tool to encourage creative individualism rather to than control it.

There was no better example of this combination of technology, individualism, and art, than Steve himself.

While Steve had been away, the Altair company had produced a computer which enthusiasts could build themselves. It came in a box which contained all the parts needed to build your own 'personal' computer. It was a very simple machine and couldn't do very much. But Steve and Woz saw possibilities for developing the idea.

The production of the Altair arrived at more or less the same time as two other important changes. The first was the release of a new magazine called Popular Mechanics which had a picture of the Altair on its first front cover. The second was the creation of PCC (the People's Computer Company) who used the sentence, "Computer power to the people," to describe its beliefs.

PCC was more of a club than a company. Its members would meet for dinner and discuss ideas. Two of these, Gordon French and Fred Moore decided to form the Homebrew Computer Club. This would be a place where people could concentrate more on developing personal computers rather than just having general discussions about communication technology.

Woz began going to the meetings, which were held in

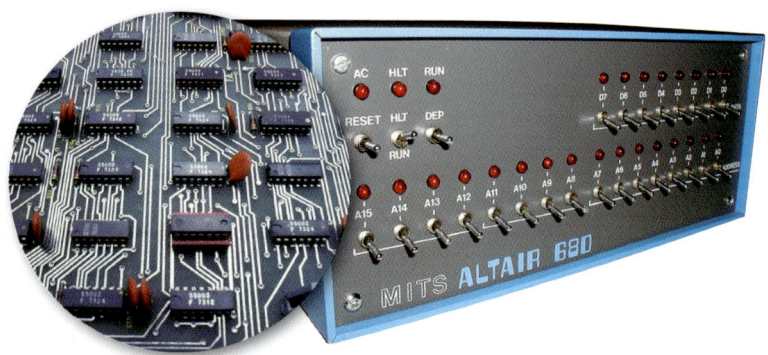

Gordon French's garage. Here, they studied the way that the Altair computer worked and how it could be made better. At one of these meetings, Woz saw a paper which described a microprocessor*. A microprocessor is a small piece of silicon*, called a 'chip', or 'microchip'. Electricity travels extremely well through silicone. It travels along thin lines of metal placed on its top surface. This is like a path that the electricity has to follow. The path is called an integrated circuit*. Before silicon chips were invented, computers were a lot bigger. Only very large companies or government departments had the space to use them. By using silicon chip technology, computers could be made a lot smaller. The Altair computer was one of the first examples of these.

But there were still problems. The Altair computer was just a box operated by switches. There was no keyboard*and no screen* although they could show simple information when attached to a TV screen.

After Woz had studied the microprocessor information, he suddenly pictured a screen, keyboard, and computer standing together on a single desk. He realised that such a 'desktop'* system should be possible to build and he started working on the project right away.

Steve was excited by Woz's idea. With his encouragement* and support, Woz worked day and night for two months. Finally, he was ready to test the result. He placed a keyboard, screen, and computer on his desk and got ready to type out a few letters. He felt nervous as he pressed the first key. But it worked. The letter was immediately shown on the screen in front of him. It was Sunday, June 29th, 1975, and Woz had made history. He was the first person to type a letter on a keyboard and see it come up on a desktop screen in front of him.

• • •

One of the problems of the Altair, and other early small computers, was that the scientific language they used for instructions was very limited. But this, too, was changing. Two electronics engineers -- Bill Gates and Paul Allen - had just completed their design of a new computer language, called 'BASIC', which could be used on the Altair. This allowed the computer to do a lot more things.

Woz and other members of the Homebrew Club were using BASIC for free because they believed that all computer knowledge should be shared. Bill Gates did not agree and sent an angry letter to the club asking them to either pay or stop using his system. Steve, too, did not share Woz's opinion that all computer information should be shared. He told Woz not to give away the secrets of the computer system he was designing. They should work on both building and selling it themselves.

Woz had never thought of making money from his computer system. But when Steve told him it would be fun to try, he agreed – just to see what would happen. Steve was the one who made it possible. Because they didn't have much money, he called local technology companies, told them he was a poor engineering student, and asked them for free parts. Woz was far too shy to do anything like this and didn't think they would have much success. He was wrong. Steve's plan worked and they got most of the parts they needed for free.

But they still needed more money, so Steve sold his car and Woz sold his scientific calculator. He was working for Hewlett Packard at the time but was only earning enough to live on. In the end, Steve and Woz managed to raise $1,300. It was enough to produce a few machines.

They built them in Steve's father's garage. Paul had given it to them to use for as long as necessary. Clara, too, had allowed the house to be used as a place to store electronic parts.

Steve said they should form their own company. Woz agreed, but he still wanted to continue working for

Hewlett Packard. Steve decided to call their new company 'Apple' - a reminder of his time at the All One Farm in Oregon. They called Woz's machine the 'Apple I' because they knew that, if it was successful, a better one would soon follow. They asked an older friend, Ron Wayne, to join the company because he had business experience. Ron said yes but left a short time later because he was scared of losing money. It was probably the worst decision of his life.

• • •

The Apple I was a lot more advanced than the Altair. A

keyboard and screen could be attached to it but it still looked like a flat box. Luckily, a few technical stores in the area were interested and Steve and Woz managed to sell enough to make a small profit. The main customers were technology enthusiasts and computer clubs rather than the general public.

Steve wanted their next machine – the 'Apple II' – to contain both electronic circuits and a keyboard in one simple design. In this way it would attract a wider market. Their main problem was money. They would need a lot more to build the Apple II.

To attract investors*, they would first need to build an example of their new machine. Woz began work on it right away.

By early September, 1976, the 'Apple II' was ready. Computer and keyboard were now part of one device. They took it to an event called the Personal Computer

Festival. Late one night, they tried it out in one of the business rooms in the hotel where they were staying. The room had a large colour television and was the best place to test their new machine. Woz attached it to the TV and pressed a button on the keyboard. A letter immediately appeared on the screen. The Apple II worked perfectly. He and Steve were very happy.

Steve approached one of his old bosses at Atari, Nolan Bushnell. Bushnell said he wasn't interested but he gave Steve the name of someone else who might be. His name was Mike Markkula. He was only thirty-three but had already retired after making a lot of money working for the company Intel. Steve called Markkula and they arranged a meeting.

Both Steve and Woz liked Markkula. He seemed fair and decent and was enthusiastic about their new machine. He and Steve wrote a business plan together. When it was finished, Markkula agreed to invest $250,000 of his own money in the company. He, Steve, and Woz would each own 26% of Apple. The rest of the shares* would be available for anyone else who wanted to invest. There was only one condition. Woz had to leave his job at Hewlett Packard and work for Apple full time.

At first, Woz said no. He was happy in his job and thought he could continue working part time for Apple. He didn't want to be a manager in a company where he had to tell other people what to do.

Neither Steve nor Markkula could make him change his mind. Finally, Allen Baum, an old friend from the Homebrew Computer Club, told Woz that joining Apple full time didn't mean that he had to become a manager. He could continue as an engineer. In the end, Woz agreed.

He left his old job at the end of 1976 and joined Apple full time.

Apple became a corporation* on January 3rd, 1977. It was now called The Apple Computer Company. Its logo*, designed by an advertising company art director called Rob Janoff, was a coloured apple with a bite taken out of it. With Markkula's money, Apple could now rent offices, employ more people, and begin production.

The Apple II was introduced at the West Coast Computer Fair in April, 1977. It was a great success.

The world's first truly personal computer had finally arrived.

Young and Difficult

"Steve was too tough on people."
(Steve Wozniak)

Income from sales of Apple II reached $770,000 by the end of 1977. It was a good start and Steve could now afford to move out of his parent's house and into a place of his own. He rented a house in Cupertino with his friend Dan Kottke. Chrisann Brennan also moved in for a while. She and Steve had continued a strange kind of relationship since the summer of 1972. Sometimes they were together as a couple, at other times they were just friends.

Since early 1975, Chrisann had been going out with a boy called Gregg Calhoun. But after travelling to India together they had broken up. She'd then asked Steve if she could move in with him and Dan for a while. Steve had said yes. Within a few weeks, they had become lovers again, but this time the result was more serious: Chrisann got pregnant.

When she told Steve, he refused to believe he was the father. This upset Chrisann and their relationship gradually got worse. Robert Friedland, the owner of the All One Farm, came to Chrisann's rescue. He suggested that she return with him to the farm and have the baby there. Chrisann agreed.

She gave birth to a baby girl on May 17th, 1978. She and Steve had been communicating with each other during her stay at the farm and he went up to Oregon to help choose a name for the baby. In the end, they decided to call her Lisa. But naming the baby didn't mean Steve was ready to take responsibility for his daughter. Once her name was chosen, he went straight back to Apple.

"Steve didn't want to have anything to do with Lisa or me," Chrisann said later.

He also refused to give Chrisann money to support her child and she had to ask for help from the government.

About a year after Lisa was born, Steve had a test to find out if he was really her father. The test was 94% positive. The courts ordered Steve to pay $385 a month to support his child. He became more generous and found a house for Chrisann and Lisa to live in without paying rent. He also paid for Lisa's school.

Despite this, he still told everyone that he doubted she was really his child.

Years later, Steve would feel sorry about the way he behaved. "If I could do it again," he said, "I would do a better job."

• • •

Steve's behaviour at work also upset a lot of people. He was particularly rude to some of Apple's new employees, two of whom were Woz's friends. He would walk into their offices, take a quick look at their work and tell them it was no good without giving them a chance to explain what they were doing. For Steve, things were either wonderful or terrible. There was no middle way. If he couldn't see that something was brilliant immediately, he rejected it as rubbish.

There also the problem of Steve's refusing to take showers because he believed his fruit and vegetable diet made it unnecessary to wash more than once a week. He would arrive at meetings with dirty feet and no shoes. Nobody could stand sitting near him.

Neither Woz nor Markkula wanted to face Steve over these problems. Both men hated arguments. Finally, Markkula suggested they employ an old friend of his from a previous company to manage Apple. His name was Mike Scott but everyone called him 'Scotty'. At first, Steve was against the idea but when Markkula told him he was still too young to run a company, he saw the truth in this and agreed.

Scotty was a big man who had no problem facing difficult situations. After Steve had upset someone unnecessarily, Scotty would take him for a walk and try to make him see that his behaviour was unacceptable. This didn't always work, and Steve and Scotty would often shout at each other. In the end, Scotty had some success in making Steve behave more reasonably. He even managed to persuade him to shower more often. But Steve still occasionally went back to his old habits and Scotty would have to talk to him again.

• • •

Following his experiences with Chrisann and Scotty, Steve began to behave a little more responsibly. Outside work, he was supporting Chrisann by sending her money every month. At Apple, he was looking more like a modern businessman. He'd had his hair cut, was now taking a shower every day and wore more appropriate clothing. He had stopped taking drugs and was going less often to Buddhist and other spiritual centres. He had also bought a new house in a place called Los Gatos.

All this was possible because of the continuing success of Woz's Apple II. The computer's sales had risen from 2,500 in 1977, to 210,000 in 1981. But Steve knew Apple II couldn't be successful forever.

His hopes were on Apple III. Woz didn't want to work on this new computer. Most of Apple's money was coming from his Apple II machine. He was happy to continue improving it, so Steve managed the Apple III project himself.

His idea was to make the Apple III do a lot more things than Woz's machine. To do this, it needed many more parts.

Once again, Steve's difficult nature proved unhelpful. After deciding on the size of the Apple III, he wouldn't listen to the engineers who told him it was too small to contain the parts necessary to make the machine he wanted. In the end, he got the size he wanted, with the result that the machine developed a lot of problems because the parts were too close together. This happened in May, 1980, after the company began sending it to stores. As a result, it was a total failure.

Similar things happened with his next project. This was to build an even more powerful computer. He decided to call it Lisa, after his daughter. By now, two other excellent technicians had joined Apple. Their names were Bill Atkinson and Jeff Raskin. In his usual extreme way, Steve recognised Atkinson's brilliance but not Raskin's. Later, he would find out that his judgement had been wrong. For now, he only wanted to work with Atkinson.

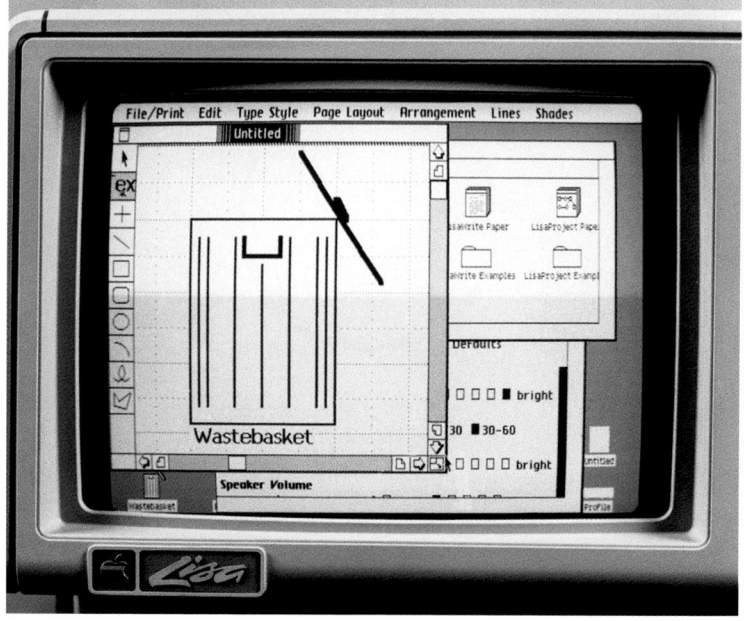

This wasn't easy. A man called John Crouch was managing the Lisa project and he was Atkinson's boss. Steve totally ignored this fact and took over the project himself. Crouch was furious and complained to Markkula.

Markkula was tired of the trouble Steve was causing, so he took him away from the Lisa project completely and gave control back to Crouch.

Steve was upset and felt he'd been treated badly. The only satisfaction he might have got came when Lisa came out two years later. Like Apple III, it was a failure. It was too expensive and had been produced for large organisations rather than consumers*.

This time Steve knew it wasn't his fault. He had seen Lisa differently. If he had behaved better he might have got the machine he wanted. Steve may have looked as if he had more ability as a manager, but underneath his difficulties in dealing with people remained.

The Macintosh Computer

"The goal was never to beat the competition or to make a lot of money. It was to do the greatest thing possible." (Andy Hertzfeld)

During the time Steve had been working on the Lisa project, an important development had taken place in the computer world. Jeff Raskin had told him that the company Xerox had managed to produce graphics* on their computer screens rather than just numbers, letters, and signs. This meant that coloured pictures and icons* could appear on screen. The information they contained could be found by using a mouse* to click* on top of the icon. The system was called a graphical user interface*, or GUI*. If Apple could find out how they were doing this, they could do the same, only better. Luckily, Xerox wanted something from Apple, too. They wanted to buy a large number of shares in the company. Steve made an agreement with them. They could buy $1 million worth of shares if they would open one of their computers and explain how their GUI system worked. Xerox agreed, but several of their managers were unhappy about giving their secrets away.

When Steve went to Xerox with Jeff Raskin in late 1979, the company tried to trick them by giving them only a small amount of information. Steve realised what they were doing and complained to the company's head office. They told him they would fix the problem and asked him to return in a few day's time. For the next visit,

Steve took Bill Atkinson and a few other top engineers with him. This time they were shown everything. Steve and Bill were very excited. Now they knew how Xerox's system worked, Bill was sure he could do an even better job.

Did Steve feel guilty about using another company's technology? No, was the answer. When asked about it, Steve replied with Picasso's famous phrase, "Good artists copy. Great artists steal."

• • •

When Apple finally became a public company on December 12th, 1980, Xerox's one million shares were worth $17.6 million. Steve's shares in the company had also risen. At the age of only twenty-five, he was now worth $256 million.

Despite the money Xerox made, most people thought Steve and Apple had got most out of the agreement. Bill Atkinson had greatly improved their GUI system and it would be an important part of the company's next big project – the Macintosh computer.

The idea was originally Jeff Raskin's. He wanted to make a cheap computer for the general public where computer, keyboard and screen would be one complete device. He wanted to call it, 'The Macintosh' after his favourite apple.

Steve loved the idea, but not the limitation of making it cheap. He just wanted what he called "a great product" without worrying about cost. Raskin disagreed. This meant that he and Steve had problems right from the beginning.

With Steve no longer working on the Lisa project, Markkula sent him to join Raskin's team. The star of the

team was a blond engineer called Burrell Smith who was almost as good as Woz. Steve also got Bill Atkinson to work on the project.

Right from the start, Steve's aggressive manner began causing problems. He called many of the things Raskin's engineers were working on "worthless" or "stupid". He was particularly bothered by the fact that Raskin's computer couldn't properly manage the GUI system Atkinson had developed. Atkinson, of course, supported Steve. This angered Raskin even more. The final break up between Steve and Raskin happened after Steve cancelled a talk Raskin was supposed to give to the company on the Macintosh. Raskin was furious and sent an angry note to Mike Scott.

Scotty called Raskin and Steve to his office. In the end, Raskin and Steve agreed that it was impossible for them to work together. On this occasion, Scotty took Steve's side and told Raskin to take some time off work until they could find something else for him to do.

Steve was then put in full control of what was now called 'The Mac'. He hired one of the engineers Woz had working on the Apple II. His name was Andy Hertzfeld. For the first time, Woz, too, got interested. Unfortunately, something happened that would change his life forever.

One day in February, 1981, Woz was injured in a private plane crash while taking off from Santa Cruz Sky Park. He was lucky to survive. He couldn't remember what had happened and spent several days in hospital until his memory recovered. After he was released, he took a long holiday from Apple and went back to Berkeley College to finish his degree. From that time on, he would only ever work for Apple part time.

Soon after Woz's accident, Mike Scott also left Apple. His behaviour had become more aggressive and he had developed some serious health problems. Markkula suggested it would be better for everyone if he left the company and Scotty agreed.

This gave Steve even more power to control the Mac project. He now had twenty people working on it. There were still problems with his behaviour. The only person who could handle his aggressiveness was Ann Bower. She had joined Apple from Intel as a human resources director.

After Steve had unnecessarily upset one of the engineers, she would go to his office and tell him, calmly, that his behaviour was not appropriate. Steve respected her and took notice of what she said, at least for a while.

But even Ann could do little to control Steve's perfectionism. Every day, he began demanding more and more from the Mac team. Everything had to be perfect, including the appearance of the finished product. Steve even criticised the look of the electronics inside the computer.

"But no one will ever know what they look like," one of the engineers told him.

"Yes, but we'll know," Steve replied. It was a lesson he had learnt from his father – to do everything as well as you can, even though people won't see it.

Some of the things Steve asked the team to do seemed totally impractical. "He changed reality to suit himself," said Bill Atkinson, "But, in the end, Steve was right. The world got a better result."

Larry Kenyon, one of Mac's engineers, later gave a good example of how Steve got people to do what seemed impossible. He was working on the system which starts the software*. One day Steve walked into his office and complained that it was taking too long to come on screen. When Larry tried to explain the reason, Steve wouldn't listen. All he said was, "If it could save a person's life, would you find a way to make it work faster?"

The example Steve gave was effective. Within a few days, Larry had got the computer's software to start twenty-eight seconds faster.

The result of Steve's obsession with perfection was that the team began to share his enthusiasm. "He thought of himself as an artist," said Andy Hertzfeld. "He encouraged the design team to think of themselves that way, too."

The results pleased everyone. Debi Coleman, another of the few people prepared to stand up to Steve, later described herself as "the luckiest person in the world to have worked with him".

But trouble was approaching.

• • •

Steve and his team were so obsessed with the Mac that they hadn't fully realised the importance of an event which took place in August, 1981. This was the month in which IBM introduced its own personal computer. Steve bought one and got Apple's engineers to take it apart and look inside. They all agreed with Steve that it wasn't a very good product.

To Steve and his team, IBM was "the evil enemy". It was the kind of large corporation they connected with government control rather than individual freedom. But what they hadn't properly considered was that IBM's operating system* was used by most of the computer industry. Apple's system was different and it might take more than a brilliant computer like the Mac to get people to change.

"It took them a year to realise what had happened," Bill Gates said later.

Gates and his company, Microsoft, had been providing software for the Apple II. He thought the Mac was a great product but that its software needed improving. He and Steve reached an agreement that Microsoft would provide software applications*, such as Word and Excel for the Mac. After that, Bill Gates often came to visit Apple's offices.

Bill Gates and Steve Jobs were very different people. Unlike Steve, Bill was a good software designer, but less of a business leader. Their personalities were different, too. Bill was neither a rebel nor particularly interested in eastern spiritualism. He was rational*. Steve was more intuitive. If he felt, inside him, that something was right, he followed that feeling, even if it didn't make sense to other people.

None of the Apple team liked Bill Gates very much. He didn't seem to listen when they explained things. This gave them the idea that he thought of himself as somehow better than they were. But it would be a mistake to think of Steve and Bill as enemies. They respected each other, and although there would later be a serious break in their relationship, this respect would last throughout Steve's life.

• • •

Mike Markkula, meanwhile, was becoming increasingly unhappy in his role as president of Apple. Since Scotty had left, the stress of the job had increased. One day, his wife told him to find someone else to replace him, or leave the company. They both agreed that Steve was not the right person for the job. Even Steve recognised that. Eventually, the company decided to try and hire a man called John Sculley as president. Sculley was famous in the marketing world because of the work he had done as Pepsi Cola's marketing manager.

They contacted Sculley and he and Steve arranged a meeting. When it happened, it was like a meeting of opposites. Sometimes though, opposites attract. This is what happened at that first meeting. Later, the attraction would prove to be false. It came from both men wanting

43

to like each other because of the position of respect each had in their different fields of business. This made them almost blind to their differences. Later, Steve would blame himself for not having seen this more clearly.

At first, however, their relationship was almost like father and son. Sculley was pleased by the admiration Steve gave him but was still not sure about joining Apple. What changed his mind was a question Steve asked him one day, which has since become one of his most famous remarks: "Do you want to spend the rest of your life selling sugared water," Steve asked, "or do you want a chance to change the world?"

At that point, Sculley agreed to become Apple's new president. The price was high. He wanted to be paid $1 million a year, and a further $1 million on signing the agreement. Apple said yes, and in April, 1983, John Sculley became their new president.

•   •   •

Nine months later, the Macintosh Computer project was finished. During that time, IBM's share of the personal computer market had grown enormously. It was now being helped by Bill Gates's decision to produce GUI software for IBM's personal computers. Steve was furious, but it was partly his own fault. Gates had asked Apple to accept Microsoft's software applications such as Word and Excel as one complete software product that would come with the Mac at a small extra cost. Steve had refused and wanted to buy them separately. After that, Gates had begun selling his software to IBM.

The two men met in Apple's offices. Steve started shouting at Bill for stealing his idea. Bill remained calm.

He reminded Steve of what he himself had done with Xerox. Underneath, Steve knew he was right. It was him, after all, who had believed in the idea that, "Good artists copy. Great artists steal."

• • •

The Macintosh Computer was launched* on January 24th, 1984. One of Steve's strengths was his ability to present products to an audience. As with everything else he did, the sound, lighting and all the other details had to be perfect. The launch was helped enormously by a sixty second video advertisement designed by Lee Clow, the creative director of the Chiat/Day Advertising Agency in Los Angeles. The video was directed by Ridley Scott, the famous director. It showed a female runner with a large hammer* being chased by the police. It was set at some time in the future where – like George Orwell's book, 1984 – everything and everyone on the video looked as if they were being controlled by the government. The video ended with the girl throwing the hammer through a large screen where the government's leader, or 'Big Brother', was giving a speech to his people. The idea behind the ad was that the new Macintosh was rebelling against the control of governments and corporations, like IBM. At the end of the ad a voice said, "On January 24th, Apple will introduce the Macintosh. And you'll see why 1984 won't be like '1984'."

It was huge success. Two important magazines, TV Guide and Advertising Age, described it as "the greatest commercial of all time."

C H A P T E R   7

Steve's Fall

"It's me or Steve. Who do you vote for?"
(John Sculley)

Following the success of the Macintosh launch, sales were good. After the failure of Lisa, everyone was happy. But the situation didn't last. The computer began to develop a number of problems. There was no fan* inside the machine because Steve thought it made an unpleasant noise. As a result, there was nothing to cool the electronic parts so they sometimes broke down. The computer also wasn't powerful enough to run some of the graphics programs at a reasonable speed. It was also seen as too expensive.

In the second half of 1984, sales began to drop. Steve and Sculley blamed each other. Steve thought Sculley had set the price too high because he only cared about making money. Sculley thought Steve's obsession over small details like the noise a fan made was the main reason for the failure.

The situation between them got worse and this worried the company's board* of directors. They told Steve to be less critical and Sculley to act with more authority. None of this advice helped. Steve continued to attack Sculley as someone who knew nothing about computers and had no idea about how Apple's products were created.

In return, Sculley continued to complain about Steve's aggressive behaviour without having the courage to do anything about it.

As Macintosh sales continued to fall, Steve's behaviour

got worse. He blamed everyone but himself for the situation. His rudeness to others got so bad that, in the end, Sculley finally told him to leave the Macintosh project altogether. Steve became angry, so Sculley went to the board. They supported Sculley. But Steve would not accept their decision and tried to make Sculley put him back on the Macintosh project. Sculley, who was due to go on a trip to China, refused. Steve then told those that still supported him that he would persuade the board to get rid of Sculley while he was away. Unfortunately for Steve, Sculley found out what he was planning and cancelled his trip.

For once, he spoke to Steve directly. "It's come to my attention that you'd like to throw me out," Sculley said.

"I think you're bad for Apple," Steve replied.

Another board meeting was held. During the meeting, Sculley suddenly asked the board to vote on who they supported. It was a clever decision. Steve and the board members were taken by surprise. With little time to think, most of them supported Sculley.

"I guess I know where things stand," Steve said, and left the room.

• • •

After the board's decision, Steve went to Europe with his girlfriend at the time, Tina Redse. They hired a car, drove around Tuscany and spent time admiring the beautiful buildings of Florence.

They also stayed in Paris. One night, he and Tina were standing on a bridge over the River Seine. It was a beautiful night and Tina suggested that they both stay in France. Steve had more than enough money to support them for the rest of their lives. He was tired of Sculley and Apple, so why didn't they buy a cottage somewhere in the countryside and live a life free of stress? But Steve said no. He was still too ambitious to retire from the computer business. That ambition, he now realised, might have to be achieved outside Apple.

He and Tina returned to California at the end of August. On September 17th, 1985, Steve sent the board a letter saying he was leaving the company from that date. He never spoke to Sculley again.

• • •

The summer of 1985 had been a bad time for Steve. There was, however, one happy experience which would take his mind off Apple and his problems with John Sculley for a while. It happened when Steve went to visit Alan Kay, one of the graphic designers at Xerox. Kay had become a friend and, knowing of Steve's interest in animation, suggested that they go and see an old friend of his, Ed Catmull, who ran the computer department at George Lucas's animation studios. Lucas was the creator of Star Wars and a man Steve admired. His company, Lucasfilm, was run by John Lasseter, an animation enthusiast who would also become a close friend of Steve's. Lucasfilm studios made hardware and software for producing digital* pictures. But George Lucas needed to sell the company because he had to raise money to pay for an expensive divorce.

Steve loved the studios and the work that Catmull and a colleague called Alvy Ray Smith were doing. He offered to buy the company for $5 million with an investment of a further $5 million. This was much less than Lucas was asking but he needed to sell quickly so they began to discuss what each thought was a fair price.

Agreement was reached in January, 1986. Instead of buying the whole company for $10 million, Steve would own 70% of it, with the rest divided between Lucasfilm's employees. They gave the company a new name, 'Pixar', taken from the name of the computers which produced their digital animation pictures. Steve let Catmull and Smith run Pixar while he concentrated on his next big project.

• • •

Since visiting a science department at Brown University in 1983, Steve had become interested in the idea of building a more powerful computer that university and other science departments could use that also wasn't too expensive. He would call his new company NeXT and that word with the small letter 'e' between the three large letters would become the company's logo.

Steve knew he needed good engineers, so he persuaded five of Apple's best employees to join his new company. When the Apple board found out, they were angry and

accused Steve of stealing both their employees and company secrets. Steve replied that the employees had decided to leave anyway because they were disappointed with Sculley's management. The board weren't satisfied and wanted to take legal action. In the end, they solved the disagreement without going to court. Steve had to agree to sell NeXT computers only to colleges and universities and not use Apple's operating system.

Things went wrong with NeXT almost from the start. Again, Steve's obsession with perfect design made things difficult for his engineers. He wanted the NeXT computer to be in the form of a cube*. This meant the electronic circuits had to be placed on top of each other. This caused heating problems because they were too close together. The cube was also difficult to make because Steve wanted it to be perfectly smooth without any production lines on its surface.

He then spent a lot of money building a modern factory where the computers would be made by machines rather than people.

Steve wanted Bill Gates to write software for the new computer and invited him to the factory for demonstrations. Each time, Bill left feeling disappointed. He thought the computer's cube case was far too expensive and that the machine didn't work properly. "When enough people want to buy your computer, I'll think about making the software," he told Steve. These visits usually ended with the two men arguing. Beneath their disagreements there was a big difference in their view of what a computer should be. Gates preferred an 'open' system. This meant that different companies could make machines and software that worked well with each other. Steve preferred a 'closed' system which was better than any other and didn't need to work well with other products.

In 1988, Steve seemed to change his mind about this when he suggested to IBM that they use his software instead of Microsoft's. He was still annoyed at Bill Gates for refusing to work for NeXT. By now, Steve's company had developed advanced software called NeXTSTEP. and he knew this was something IBM were interested in. When Bill Gates found out what Steve was doing, he was furious. He told IBM they would be making a big mistake if they bought Steve's software. But this made no difference to IBM. They, and other computer companies, were still interested in buying NeXTSTEP. However, for IBM there was one condition: for them to buy the software, Steve would have to agree to stop producing computers. Steve refused and the agreement collapsed.

The launch of the NeXT computer took place in a concert hall in San Francisco on October 12th, 1988. There was an audience of three thousand, including a lot of important university people. As always, Steve gave a wonderful presentation but it had some nasty surprises. Worst of all was the cost of the computer: $6,500. The university people were shocked. They understood that Steve had promised to keep the price between $2,500 to $3,000. They also found out that the computer would not be ready until the middle of 1989.

When the computer finally came out in the summer of that year, its sales were only 4% of what the company had expected. It was a disaster and production would finally stop two years later. Steve would describe that moment as the lowest point of his professional career.

CD2
1

Romance and Family

"Mona is my family. I can't imagine a better sister."
(Steve Jobs)

Since his break up with Chrisann in 1978, Steve had had a number of other relationships. The first serious one was with an employee at Mckenna's - the company responsible for advertising Apple's first products. Her name was Barbara Jasinski. They went to music concerts together, took holidays in Hawaii, and eventually shared a house in the Santa Cruz mountains. Their relationship lasted for four years. It ended in 1982, shortly after Steve met the famous singer, Joan Baez, who had once been Bob Dylan's girlfriend. Joan was forty-one, Steve was twenty-seven. At first, the difference in their ages was not important and they soon became lovers. Dan Kottke's girlfriend, Elizabeth Holmes, thought that Steve was particularly attracted to Joan because of the connection with Bob Dylan.

Joan had a fourteen-year-old son called Gabriel from her former husband, David Harris. Steve found out she'd been teaching him to type so he gave Gabriel an Apple II computer. He also gave Joan a Macintosh. One day, he was showing her how it could produce music and played an example. But when he told her that computers would eventually sound better than humans playing music, Joan got upset. To her, the idea was terrible.

Steve wanted children of his own, so when he realised that Joan didn't want to have any more, he knew their relationship wouldn't last. Their romance ended after three years but they remained good friends.

He was with Joan when he met his next girlfriend. Her name was Jennifer Egan. She was a student at the University of Pennsylvania. Steve sat next to her at a dinner party he and Joan had been invited to. By that time, Steve and Joan were no longer going out together.

Jennifer had been working for a newspaper over the summer holidays. She and Steve talked about things of interest in the news. He found her interesting and attractive. The next day, he called her at the newspaper's office and they began going out together.

It wasn't an easy relationship. Jennifer thought Steve was being dishonest by telling her not to become too fond of material objects while making computers that he wanted people to buy. Their relationship finished in 1984, when Jennifer felt she was still too young to get married.

A few months later, Steve met someone he would later describe as, "the most beautiful woman I'd ever seen." One day, early in 1985, he was visiting the offices of the Apple Foundation. It gave Apple computers to organizations that didn't work for profit and helped less fortunate people. Sitting in one of the offices was a beautiful blonde-haired woman. Steve had been passing by the open door. When he saw her, he stopped, went in and introduced himself. The woman's name was Tina Redse. Steve asked Tina out but she said no. She was living with her boyfriend and didn't want her life to change. But Steve wouldn't give up and asked her again. This time she agreed. They went for a long walk in a park and found they had similar views about many things. They began dating and within a few months were living together.

Tina could understand the pain Steve felt at being

abandoned as a child. She, too, came from a difficult family and her life as a child had not been easy. They were both left feeling different from other people, as if they didn't connect with the rest of the world.

This brought them closer together. Not caring what others thought, they showed their love quite openly. Employees at NeXT still remember how physically romantic they were, even in the company's reception area.

They remembered the fights, too. These could happen quite suddenly. It didn't matter where they were: in restaurants, cinemas, company offices. Their anger was as strong as their love and they didn't care who knew it.

They were quieter during the time of Steve's problems with Sculley and Apple. Tina was a great support for him at this time. Twenty-five years after they separated, Tina sent Steve an email reminding him of the time they spent together in Paris and the moment that could have changed their lives.

"I tried to get you to begin a new life with me in Paris," Tina wrote. "I wanted us to live simple lives where I could cook you simple dinners and we could be together every day. I like to think you considered it before you laughed and said "What could I do? I've made myself unemployable."

After they returned to California, the up and down nature of their relationship continued. Tina didn't like living in Steve's house because there was hardly any furniture in it. He was such a perfectionist he could never find anything he liked enough to buy. The house was uncomfortable in other ways, too. Steve had hired a young couple to cook and clean for him and they made Tina feel unwelcome.

There were other differences between them. One of these was Steve's idea that people could be taught good artistic sense. "Steve believed it was our job to teach people what they should like," she remembered. Tina disagreed and felt that love of beauty was an individual quality.

She was also puzzled by Steve's coldness. Unlike Tina, he never gave money to poor people in the street or was much interested in helping others less fortunate than himself. It wasn't because he was mean; he was just too focused on his own world to think of these things.

These differences caused fierce arguments which often ended with Tina returning to her apartment in Los Altos. When she'd been away for more than a few days, Steve would miss her terribly. In the end, he asked her to marry him. Tina said no. Living with Steve was too similar to the explosive atmosphere of the family home she had experienced as a child.

They broke up in 1989, but Steve would often miss Tina at different times throughout the rest of his life. Tina felt the same and later said, "Though it was impossible for us to have the relationship we once hoped for, the love and care I felt for him has continued."

• • •

A year after Steve left Apple, he found out that his mother, Clara, had cancer. As she was dying, Steve spent many hours beside her bed and talked of things he had never mentioned before. During this time, Clara gave him more details about the circumstances of his adoption. Steve then decided to find out more about his real parents.

He didn't have much luck at first. The doctor who had

signed his birth records told him that all information about his real parents had been destroyed in a fire. This was not true and the doctor wrote a letter containing the information Steve needed. He had told his lawyer to deliver the letter to Steve after his death. He died soon after Steve had contacted him and the letter arrived a few days later. Steve didn't do anything at first because he didn't want to upset Paul or Clara. But after Clara died, in early 1986, he succeeded in finding his real mother.

Her name was now Joanne Simpson. She was living in Los Angeles and Steve went to visit her. Joanne became very emotional when they met. She told Steve that her father had made her sign the adoption papers but that she did so only when she was sure that he was happy with his new parents. She apologized over and over again and told Steve how much she had missed him over the years. Steve was understanding and told her not to worry. But he never felt truly close to her.

Joanne then told him about her life after the adoption. She and Abdulfattah had married soon after her father died. They had another child, a girl called Mona, who was Steve's sister. Five years later, Abdulfattah abandoned the family and Joanne met and married a man called George Simpson. Although that marriage didn't last long either, Joanne and Mona kept Simpson's name.

Steve was very excited by the thought of having a sister. He was keen to discover all he could about her. Joanne told him that she was a writer and lived in New York. She had never told Mona that she had a brother, but on the day of Steve's visit she telephoned her and gave her the news. She didn't tell Mona who her brother was, only that he was rich, famous, and good-looking.

Joanne and Steve then went to New York where they had arranged to meet Mona in the St Regis Hotel. When they met, Mona and Steve got along with each other immediately. They took a long walk together and talked about their lives.

"He was lovely," Mona remembered. "Just a normal, sweet guy."

Steve's relationship with his sister would be one of the closest in his life. Soon after they met, Mona tried to find out where Abdulfattah was living because she wanted her and Steve to meet him. Steve wasn't interested. "He didn't treat me well," he later explained, but what Steve found hardest to forgive was the fact that he had abandoned Mona. When Mona said she was going to see Abdulfattah anyway, Steve told her not to mention him.

Steve was more forgiving towards Joanne and they met, together with Mona, several times over the years. But his real father was never mentioned. It was as if he had never existed.

• • •

After his separation from Tina, Steve probably felt he would never marry and build a family with someone he loved. He'd had a number of serious relationships, but none had led to marriage and family. He knew he was difficult to live with: obsessed with work, liked to argue, and often uncaring about others. The woman who could both interest and tolerate him would have to be intelligent, beautiful, strong, calm, loving, and independent. Did such a woman exist?

The answer was yes, and one Thursday evening in late October, 1989, she walked into a talk Steve was giving at the Stanford Business School. Her name was Laurene Powell. A friend had persuaded her to go to the talk, but by the time they arrived all the seats were taken. Laurene was brave enough to sit in one of the reserved seats at the front of the room. Steve arrived and as he was waiting to begin his talk, sat next to her. When he asked who she was, Laurene gave him her name and joked that she'd won the seat in a contest and that the main prize was that he would take her out for dinner.

The last thing Steve had expected that day was to meet a beautiful woman with a good sense of humour. Unfortunately, there wasn't time to get to know her better because he had to begin his talk.

After the talk finished, Laurene got up and made her way out of the room. Steve ran after her. "What about that dinner I'm supposed to be taking you to?" he asked. "How about Saturday?"

Laurene laughed and said OK. They left the room together and arranged to meet on Saturday afternoon. They said goodbye and Laurene went to her car. Steve suddenly turned around, ran up to her and said, "What about dinner tonight?" Again Laurene said yes and they spent the evening in a restaurant in Palo Alto.

Steve found out that Laurene was from a middle class family in New Jersey. Her father had been a pilot who had died a hero's death when the plane he'd been flying was hit by another plane. Rather than jump out to save himself, he had guided his damaged plane to an area where there were no houses so that no one was killed. The only victim was himself.

The loss of her father made Laurene very independent. When her mother's next marriage turned out to be a disaster, Laurene was able to survive in a difficult home by protecting her younger brothers as well as she could. She had done well at school and university and was doing equally well at the Stanford Business School. There was no doubt that she would find a good, well-paid job. But for Laurene, money was just a tool to help her become independent.

For the next three months, Steve and Laurene spent every free moment they had together. Then, on the first day of January, 1990, Steve asked her to marry him. She accepted. It seemed to be a new beginning for them both.

But strangely, Steve didn't appear to be in a hurry to get married. In fact, over the next few months he didn't mention marriage again at all. Finally, Laurene's best friend, Kat Smith, asked Steve if he'd changed his mind about marrying Laurene. Steve said no, but he just wanted to be sure that Laurene would be happy living with the kind of person he was. In the meantime, Laurene had become tired of waiting and in September she moved out of Steve's house.

This forced Steve to act. The following month he gave her an expensive ring and again asked her to marry him. By the end of the month, they were living together again.

At Christmas, They went to Steve's favourite holiday place: Kona Village in Hawaii. While they were there, Laurene got pregnant. Most people would probably have felt that this was a good enough reason to get married immediately. But not Steve. He still felt unsure and asked himself if he was still in love with Tina. But in the end, he decided to marry Laurene. It was the right decision. He realised that she was much better at handling the kind of person he was than Tina ever could have been.

Steve and Laurene were married in Yosemite National Park on March 18th, 1991. Both Steve's father, Paul Jobs, and his sister, Mona, came to the wedding. They were married by Steve's spiritual teacher, Kobun Chino. It was snowing at the time.

The beauty of the wedding brought joy into Steve's life at a time when he most needed it. The failure of NeXT had, for the first time, made him doubt his own intuition. But his marriage to Laurene gave every sign of providing the support he needed to recover.

That recovery, when it came, would produce the most amazing change of fortune in business history.

The Return

"Steve's the only one who can save Apple."
(Larry Ellison)

From the time Steve left Apple up until the late 1980s, the company had been able to keep its sales reasonably steady. In 1987, John Sculley felt confident enough to publicly criticise Steve by announcing, "Apple will never be a consumer products company. Advanced technology cannot be designed and sold as a consumer product." Before too long, these words would sound embarrassing.

Steve was angry but could only watch as the company he loved took a different direction. Within ten years it would lead to the collapse of Apple as the world's most creative computer company.

• • •

By the time the NeXT computer came out, Microsoft was almost ready to release its Windows software. It was launched in 1990 under the name 'Windows 3.0'. It had used a lot of Apple's GUI technology and was immediately successful with sales of around 10 million in its first two years.

With most PCs using Windows 3.0, Apple suffered even more. Things got worse as Microsoft continued to improve their Windows operating system. Windows 3.1 came out in 1992 and was followed, three years later, by Windows 95, which became the most successful operating system ever.

Apple began to collapse. During his annual Christmas holiday in Hawaii, Steve was walking along a beach with Larry Ellison, a rich friend of his. Steve was also extremely rich by this time, mainly because of the success of Pixar, so Ellison suggested they put their money together and buy Apple and put Steve back as CEO*. "I'll only go back if they ask me to," Steve replied.

By this time, the Apple board had got rid of Sculley. He'd been replaced by a man called Michael Spindler. Spindler's answer to Apple's problems was to try and sell the company to IBM or one of the other large computer companies. When that failed, the board got rid of him, too. They then hired a man called Gil Amelio as CEO.

Amelio was a pleasant, rather dull man. In Steve's opinion, he knew little about the world of computers. During 1994, his first year at Apple, they lost a billion dollars. At the time, Steve had felt bad about what was happening to his old company. One day, he called Gil and came straight to the point. "I want you to help me return to Apple," he said. "I'm the only one who can save the company."

Amelio, worried that Steve wanted to replace him as CEO, refused.

• • •

Steve didn't spend much time feeling sorry for himself. Despite the problems with NeXT, Apple had more to lose than he did. His conversation with Larry Ellison in Hawaii had only been possible because Steve was suddenly richer than he'd ever been. The reason was his other company, Pixar.

Two years after he bought Pixar, in 1986, they had

begun producing animated software for the Disney company. Michael Eisner, Disney's CEO, and Jeffrey Katzenburg, head of Disney's film department, both liked the short animated films that John Lasseter and his team at Pixar had been making. The most famous was a cartoon story called, Tin Toy, which won the Academy Award for best short animated film of 1988. Eisner wanted Lasseter to leave Pixar and come and work for Disney. Lasseter said no. He had become a close friend of Steve's over the years and believed in the work they were doing together. Instead, Lasseter and his team continued producing both hardware and software for Eisner and Katzenburg until Disney became their biggest customer.

The relationship between the two companies had been working well and, one day in 1991, Katzenburg had invited Steve down to the Disney film studios in Burbank. He wanted him to look at the results of the work the two companies had been doing together.

During his tour of the studios, Steve suddenly asked Katzenburg, "Is Disney happy with Pixar?".

"Of course," Katzenburg replied.

"And do you think that Pixar is happy with Disney?"

Katzenburg was surprised by the question. "I suppose so," he said quietly.

"Well we're not," Steve said in his usual direct manner. "We want to do a film with you. That would make us happy."

Katzenberg liked the idea. The problem was reaching an agreement. Steve and Katzenberg had similar personalities. Both were aggressive and the talks lasted several months. But Disney had the advantage. They were a rich company, while Pixar had very little money of its own. Agreement was reached in May 1991. Disney would own the film Pixar produced and Pixar would get 12.5% of the money it earned. Steve had not been happy with the agreement but he'd been in no position to ask for a better one.

The idea for the film that John Lasseter had thought of was clear from its title: Toy Story. He wanted to make an animated film about two toys. One was old, the other was new. The new toy had become its child owner's favourite and the old toy felt jealous. Eventually the two toys would become friends when they – and all the other toys in their owner's house – were threatened by an evil child who lived next door. The old toy was called 'Woody', and the new toy was 'Buzz Lightyear'.

Lasseter and Katzenberg disagreed about the Woody character. Katzenberg wanted to make him more evil. Because Disney were providing most of the money, Lasseter was forced to agree. But when Eisner, Katzenberg and other top people from Disney saw what Lasseter had produced they didn't like it and stopped production. Lasseter told them the film wasn't working because Katzenberg had changed his original idea. He asked them to give him more time to make the film his way. They agreed but would not provide any more money.

At this point Steve came to the rescue. He supported Lasseter by giving Pixar some of his own money to make the film. When it was finished, everyone liked the result and by February 1994, Toy Story was back in production. Its release date was set for November, 1995. Steve, who was still annoyed that Pixar didn't have more control over the project, knew that only one thing could change the situation: more money. The best way to raise money quickly was by making Pixar a public company. This would allow people to buy shares. The company could then use this money to become more independent. But it was dangerous. If Toy Story failed, Steve would lose the money he had put into the film and Disney would have even more control.

On November 29th, 1995, one week after Toy Story was released, Pixar went public. Steve, and everyone else at the company were very nervous. Steve had set the price of one share at $22. Most people at Pixar thought this was too high. Steve took no notice. He'd made the right decision. Before the end of that first day, the share price had almost doubled. The success of Toy Story was beyond anyone's wildest dreams. For an investment of $50 million dollars, Steve, in less than twelve hours had made an unbelievable $1.2 billion. Suddenly Pixar was more independent, and in a position to reach a better agreement with Disney.

From then on, Michael Eisner agreed to let Pixar provide half the money for future films and take half the profits. The names Pixar and Disney would appear together in any future production.

In less time than it takes to fly from San Francisco to London, Steve had turned Pixar into a great company.

The question on many people's minds then was: could he do the same for Apple?

• • •

At the time of Pixar's success, Apple were in trouble. Sales continued to fall and in an attempt to save the situation the company had been developing a new operating system called Copland. But Copland was having too many problems and they needed to find a replacement, fast. They knew that the NeXT computer had failed, but the company's NeXTSTEP operating system was doing reasonably well. Many at Apple wanted to buy the whole of Steve's NeXT company. This would give them the software they needed. But Gil Amelio wasn't keen on dealing with Steve so he looked at other possibilities. One of these was Microsoft. Bill Gates was enthusiastic about designing software for Apple but when Gil presented all the possibilities to the board, they decided that buying NeXT made more sense.

Bill Gates was furious. "Don't you understand that Steve doesn't know anything about technology?" he shouted when Gil told him of the board's decision. "He's just a brilliant salesman. You'll never make it work on your machines."

Steve had gone to the board meeting on the day the decision had been taken. It was December 2nd, 1996, and the first time he'd walked into Apple's main offices since 1985. When he entered the boardroom he saw that Mike Markkula was still on the board. Although he'd been angry at Markkula when he'd supported Sculley back in 1985, Steve walked over and shook his hand to show there was no bad feeling.

This time, Markkula was on Steve's side and had supported the decision to buy NeXT. However, it wasn't clear exactly what role Steve would now have within Apple.

"Do you want to just take the money for NeXT and leave?" Gil asked, when they met in his office.

Steve replied that he was too tired to give an answer. Gil insisted, so Steve suggested he become an advisor to the chairman*. The chairman was Ed Woolard, another supporter of Steve's, but they hadn't yet met. Gil was happy Steve hadn't said "CEO" so he agreed.

Steve Jobs returned to Apple in January, 1997. His feelings were mixed. On one hand he was happy to be back, but on the other he was upset by not being asked to join the board.

Gil Amelio introduced Steve to the rest of the employees in Apple's large presentation room. As Steve walked on stage, everyone clapped and cheered. It was a welcome change from Gil's boring talk which had lasted for almost three hours. The short talk Steve gave was full of energy and enthusiasm. He told them that Apple had lost its magic and it was up to him and everyone else in the room to put it back.

In the weeks that followed it became clear that Steve was acting as more than an advisor. The first thing he did was to put the people from NeXT he trusted most into important positions. Then he began to look at all the different products Apple were working on. It was worse than he thought. There were far too many projects, and 'Newton', the one they were spending most time on, Steve hated. It was a machine you could hold in your hand which recognised handwriting and needed a stylus* to make it work. Steve hated styluses. He preferred touch screens*, operated by the fingers.

He walked into Gil's office one day and told him to get rid of Newton.

"Steve, do you know how expensive that will be?"

"It doesn't matter. Just get rid of it. People will thank you in the end."

Gil tried to keep the Newton project going but the board supported Steve and in May, 1997, Newton was abandoned.

It was becoming increasingly clear to Ed Woolard and the rest of the board that Gil Amelio was unable to manage the company properly. Woolard wanted to make Steve CEO, but for the time being, the board decided to keep him as a more active advisor. Gil, however, lost his job.

Steve, who quite liked Gil as a person, called him that evening and said he was sorry about what had happened.

Gil thanked him but was still suspicious of Steve's role in his exit from the company.

Another meeting of all employees was called in the presentation room where Gil would say goodbye and Steve would accept his new position. After Gil's goodbye speech, Steve walked on stage. It was clear he was serious about saving Apple.

"What's wrong with this company?" he asked.

People looked uncomfortable. A few gave soft replies.

"It's the products," Steve shouted. "They're awful. There's just no sex in them any more."

Steve's old friend Woz was there that day, too. He had come back to Apple as a part time advisor. He was very pleased that Steve had returned to the company. "It was just what we needed," he said. "Steve knows how to bring the magic back."

Steve then turned his attention to the board. He told Woolard that they should all go, except him. "Either they leave, or I do," Steve told him. He wasn't angry at the board. After all, they had invited him back to the company. But Apple needed to break its connections with the past and he didn't want anyone to stop him doing what needed to be done.

In the end, Woolard agreed. The board members left and Steve was now in full control.

His next move surprised everyone. He made an agreement with Bill Gates.

Every year, Apple held special presentations called 'MacWorld' events. They gave the company a chance to present its new products to the world. Steve announced his agreement with Bill Gates at a MacWorld event in Boston in August, 1997.

"I'd like to announce one of our first new partnerships*
today," Steve began. "with Microsoft."

The audience gasped. Apple and Microsoft had been
fighting for years over Microsoft's use of their GUI
technology. But now, Steve explained, Apple needed their
help, especially their Word and Excel applications. Bill Gates,
despite his earlier annoyance, had always liked Apple and
had agreed to provide the software Steve needed.

He ended his presentation with the words, "We have to
get rid of the idea that for Apple to win, Microsoft has to
lose."

By the end of the day, Apple's value had risen by 33%.

• • •

Steve knew that for Apple to be successful it needed a
new public face. People thought of it as old and
unfashionable. Steve called Lee Clow, the advertising man
who had worked on the famous 1984 ad. Lee thought of
a two word phrase, "Think Different" as the best way to
give people the idea that Apple was a new force in
computing.

Steve loved the idea. The ad, when it came out, showed
pictures of famous rebels like Gandhi, John Lennon, and
Picasso with the words Think Different at the top and the
Apple logo in the corner.

Just like the 1984 ad, this, too, was a great success. It
came out in September 1997, at the same time that Steve
was finally made temporary CEO. On the same day, he
called all the employees to the presentation room and told
them they would again be concentrating on producing
"really great products."

Steve and Apple had returned to the world stage.

iMac, iPod, iPhone, iPad, iCloud

"Less is better." (Dieter Rams)

Jony Ive, head of Apple's design team, was sitting in the audience when Steve gave his talk. Jony was a thirty-year-old Englishman from north-east London who had quickly risen to one of the most important positions in the company. But he was unhappy with the management's obsession with making money rather than concentrating on creating excellent products and had decided to leave. When he heard that Steve was coming back as CEO, he went to hear what he had to say. By the end of Steve's talk, Jony had become so enthusiastic that he decided to stay with Apple and see if Steve's return made any difference.

From an early age, Jony's father had shown him how to create and build beautiful things. There was one condition: he had to first draw them by hand. His father's teaching made Jony appreciate that the most important thing about creating something good, was the care you put into the whole project.

On finishing school, Jony went to college in Newcastle. During the summer holidays, he worked at a design company. Unlike many designers, Jony also had a good knowledge of electronic engineering, so he had always appreciated the Macintosh computer. He went on to win two important awards* from the Royal Society of Arts. Both involved engineering as well as design.

After finishing college, Jony helped form a company called Tangerine, which did some work for Apple. After one of his trips to Apple's offices in Cupertino, Jony was offered a job and decided to stay. He quickly rose to the top of the design team. But with Gil Amelio in charge, he wasn't happy.

"There wasn't that feeling of putting care into a product," he later told Steve.

Steve knew exactly what he meant, but at the time he became CEO, he didn't know Jony existed. He began to look outside the company for an international designer who was well-known. But then, as he was touring the factory one day, he stopped by Jony's office for a few quick words. The 'quick words' turned into a long, enthusiastic talk. Both Steve and Jony shared the same ideas about design. The main thing they believed in was: "keep things simple." Jony particularly admired the work of the German designer, Dieter Rams, who worked for the company, Braun. Dieter's phrase "Less is better" was famous in the design world.

Steve and Jony soon became friends. They began having lunch together regularly and Steve was always going to Jony's office to discuss ideas. He was one of the few people in the company never to experience Steve's aggressive moods personally.

After a while, the two men never seemed to be apart. Almost every day, after having lunch together, Steve would spend much of the afternoon in Jony's studio. They even travelled to France together to look at examples of French design. Their families became close, too, and there were regular dinners at each other's houses. Soon, it was clear that Jony's role in creating products was at least equal to Steve's.

Jony had improved the design of Apple's PowerMac computers but the first truly different product to come out of his partnership with Steve was the iMac. This was a desktop computer which came as a complete device with keyboard, screen, and computer that could fit easily on a desk. Two other things were unusual about the iMac. Its case was green and blue, and the electronics inside could be seen through it. Its GUI was better than ever and its cost was also reasonable.

The iMac was launched on May 6th, 1998, and became the fastest selling computer in Apple's history. It was followed, a few months later, later by the iBook, a laptop* model of the iMac. The 'i' in the names of these two computers stood for 'internet'.

• • •

Even though Steve's job title was only 'temporary' CEO, he was working harder than ever. Not only that. He was also CEO of Pixar and the stress of running two companies was beginning to show. The situation was made worse when Jim McCluney, Apple's head of operations, decided he couldn't stand the stress of working for Steve any longer and left the company. For three months, Steve took over the job himself. It was too much to manage, so he began looking for a new head of operations.

The same year that the iMac was launched, Steve met Tim Cook. Tim had been an important manager with the company, Compaq Computers. He was calm, intelligent, hard working, and sensible. Steve liked him immediately and offered him the job of head of Operations. Tim accepted.

Steve's intuition had been right. Within a few months, Tim Cook had made Apple's production system a lot simpler. He did this by reducing the number of companies that supplied Apple from one hundred to twenty-four.

These twenty-four all had to move their businesses closer to Apple. He then closed several of the buildings where Apple parts were stored and made sure that everything that was needed was stored close to the Apple factory. In this way, Tim was able to reduce the production time for making computers from four months to only two.

Steve and Jony, meanwhile, were pleased with the results of their partnership and looked forward to doing many future projects together. This doesn't mean that their relationship was always sweet. But it was Jony who sometimes got annoyed with Steve rather than the other way round. He was particularly bothered when Steve accepted praise for an idea that had been his. But he also recognized the importance of Steve's role. "My ideas would have got nowhere if it wasn't for Steve," he said.

What made them so close was the belief they shared that products should be as simple to use as possible. But in order for this to happen, it was necessary to understand the product more deeply. Only by understanding what was really necessary could you get rid of what wasn't.

By 2001, it was becoming clear to Steve, Jony and others in the industry, that what was no longer necessary was the traditional role of the computer itself. Since the creation of Apple, twenty-five years earlier, the computer had always been the centre of the digital revolution. Other machines, such as small video cameras, music players and mobile phones were becoming increasingly popular. They were also making the computer look boring. The idea that Steve and Jony shared was that, from now on, computers should act as a digital centre, or hub*, through which other machines could be connected in order make them do more complicated and exciting things. But rather than focus only on computers, Apple would also make the smaller devices which connected to them. This would mean designing and producing devices with cameras, music players, cell phones and more. Again, this was part of Steve's belief that Apple should control a consumer's whole digital experience.

This idea became stronger after the company, Adobe, refused to make their video software available for the iMac. Unfortunately for them, they hadn't thought it would sell well. Steve never forgave them. From that time on, he decided never to depend on an outside company again.

This even included controlling the places where consumers could buy Apple products.

Steve wanted to put specially designed Apple stores in large shopping centres. This would make it easy and convenient for customers to buy their products. The stores would reflect Jony's design ideas. The main colour would be pure white. They would be open and simple with a central space where customers could try out products and ask questions from helpful and knowledgeable assistants. These areas would be called 'genius bars'.

The first Apple store opened on May 19th, 2001, at Tyson's Corner, in Virginia, USA. On the wall was a large picture of John Lennon and Yoko Ono lying in bed with the words, "Think Different' above their heads. Within a few years, there were Apple stores all over the world. The largest was in Covent Garden, London, UK. The one attracting the most customers was on Fifth Avenue, New York. It was visited by an average of fifty thousand customers a week.

• • •

By the early 2000's, Steve was aware that the two fastest growing areas of interest were music and photography. Music, above all, was going to offer Apple the greatest opportunity.

He had good reasons for thinking this. The music industry was suffering because services like Napster were allowing people to connect with each other through their website* and download* music for free. This method of sharing music was badly affecting the sales of CDs. It also affected the money the artists who made them earned.

Steve was against the idea of free exchange of music. He thought artists should be paid for what they created. But he also thought that the music industry had treated artists and consumers badly and that the situation needed to change. The problem for consumers was that they had to buy a whole CD even if they only liked one of the songs on it. The problem for artists was that most of them weren't paid enough. Unless they were extremely famous, they also had to create what the music industry thought would be successful.

In order to solve these problems, Steve came up with the

idea of iTunes. This would be an online* store which would allow consumers to buy only the songs or music they wanted, rather than a whole CD. Part of this money would then go to the artists responsible for creating that music.

But this was only the first step. Customers would also need a portable* music player which they could use with iTunes. For this, Jony designed the iPod which was operated by a wheel, invented by his colleague, Phil Schiller. By turning the wheel, customers could view lists of hundreds of songs at any one time and then listen to them on their iPod. It was powered by a battery but could be connected to a computer for doing more complicated things.

Steve launched the iPod on October 23rd, 2001. Other people in the industry thought that its price of $399 was too high and that few people would buy it.

Consumers proved them wrong. Not only were its sales huge, it also stood for everything that Apple valued. It was a perfect mix of art, creation, technology, and simplicity.

From that time on, these qualities would be associated with all Apple products.

• • •

For iTunes to work, Steve had had to get the music companies to agree to make the music they owned available. Because they were losing so much money through downloading, they agreed.

Bill Gates was jealous. "Steve's done it again," he said. "How did he get the music industry to agree?" He decided to ask Steve to make the iPod and iTunes store available for Windows. At first, Steve wasn't keen, but when others at Apple told him how much they could earn from this he agreed.

Only one thing now bothered Steve. His favourite band, The Beatles, were still not allowing their music to be made available on iTunes. His problems with their company, Apple Corps, went all the way back to the first days of Apple when the Beatles took legal advice over whether Steve was allowed to use their 'Apple' name for his company. These problems were finally solved in 2010 by Apple paying a large amount of money to the Beatles. After that, all their music became available on iTunes.

• • •

By 2005, the number of iPods sold was difficult to believe – an amazing twenty million. Almost half the company's entire sales were coming from iPods.

This made Steve nervous. He was particularly worried by the threat of cell phones. Already some of the newer models were including video technology and this was badly affecting sales of cameras. The same could happen with music. If it did, the iPod would be finished.

Steve's answer was to look for an agreement with a cell phone company to build iPods into their machines. He contacted the Motorola company and they agreed with the idea. But the results were disappointing. The technology didn't work properly and Steve abandoned the project.

The answer to the problem was obvious: Apple should

make their own cell phone with iPod technology included. At the time he decided this, another project was being developed by a small team at Apple. It involved designing a computer which worked by touching its screen rather than using a keyboard. This 'touch screen technology', as it was called, was perfect for devices like cell phones which also worked as cameras and music players because it meant that the screen could be a lot bigger. The keyboard would simply appear by touching the screen in a certain place when you needed it and disappear again when you didn't.

The original idea had come from one of Microsoft's engineers who had invited both Bill Gates and Steve to his birthday party. At the party, he kept telling Steve about how good his idea was. Both Bill and Steve were annoyed with him, but for different reasons. Bill was annoyed because the man was giving away company secrets, Steve was annoyed because he didn't like the technology: it used a stylus instead of a person's fingers. He knew Apple could improve the system.

Jony and his team began working on improvements straight away. It took them six months. Jony showed the results to Steve privately because he didn't want Steve to start shouting at his engineers if he didn't like what they had done.

He needn't have worried. Steve loved it. The only problem was how to stop the touch screen from working accidentally when you held it against your ear to answer a phone call, or it rubbed against something in your pocket. It took a further six months to solve that problem. The answer was to keep the screen from working until the user moved a finger quickly across it from left to right.

For the screen itself, Jony used a special kind of glass. It was amazingly strong but sensitive enough to send signals to the electronic parts from the touch of a user's fingers.

Everything was ready, but at the last minute, Steve decided he wanted to make the phone's case smaller and its screen bigger.

Jony was upset but he realised that Steve was right. He and his team worked nights and weekends to improve the design. Finally it was ready. Steve loved it. It was strong, thin, comfortable to handle, and easy to use.

With the words, "This is the best thing we've ever done," he launched the iPhone - called the 'iPhone 3GS' - at a Macworld event in San Francisco in January, 2007. "This will change everything," he went on. He then gave the audience two earlier examples. "The Macintosh changed the whole computer industry. The iPod did the same to the music industry. And this new device, the iPhone, will change communication forever.

As Steve showed the audience how the new machine worked, they stood, clapping and cheering. Could the iPhone be Apple's greatest success?

There was only one problem. The price. At $500 Apple's competitors said it was far too expensive. Few people would buy it. They had been wrong in the past, and they were wrong again. By the end of 2010, Apple had sold more than ninety million iPhones and were making more than half the money from total world sales in the cell phone market.

• • •

The success of the iPhone didn't affect the development of Apple's other new products. In 2008, they released 'MacBook Air'- advertised as "the world's thinnest laptop computer." Steve and Jony's obsession with 'thin' as the most important aspect of design also led to an improved iPhone model, the iPhone 4, which wouldn't be released until June, 2010. But what interested Jony most was the idea of replacing the laptop computer with a simple flat tablet* with a touch screen keyboard. It would be smaller, simpler, and far easier to handle than a laptop. Steve was enthusiastic and the result of their cooperation was the iPad, released in April, 2010. Three million iPads were sold in just over two months and by the end of the year it had become the fastest selling computer machine of all time.

These achievements were all the more amazing because by 2010, Steve had become very ill. Despite this, every new product seemed to give him an explosion of energy. Looking pale and thin, his voice sounded as enthusiastic as ever as he announced each of Apple's new inventions.

At times, he was still as angry, too. What bothered him most was Google's attempt to compete with the iPhone by releasing their Android model at the end of 2008. He was particularly annoyed because several of Google's management team had previously been on the Apple board. In Steve's view, they had stolen Apple's technology.

The public argument with Google again made people aware of the difference between two separate operating systems. Android used an 'open' system. This meant that it could operate other programs or applications produced by a variety of different companies. The iPhone used a 'closed' system. It would operate only programs and applications designed by Apple. This gave the company more control. Steve also had the opinion that it prevented viruses* entering and damaging the software.

Opinion was divided. Many preferred the way Apple's system worked smoothly on the iMac, iPod, iPhone, iPad or whatever device they were using. Others saw it as a worrying attempt at control. By that time, Steve had banned the use of applications he thought might have a bad effect on children or that were too politically sensitive. Many people found this strange. It seemed to go against the main thing Steve and Apple had earlier believed in: freedom of expression. The famous Apple ad of 1984 had shown an individual destroying a picture of a controlling 'Big Brother'. Wasn't Steve now behaving like that individual by controlling what was made available on Apple's machines?

In the end, Steve partly recognized the strength of that argument and allowed other applications on to Apple's iTunes store. But the Apple system still remained relatively 'closed'.

Steve's final success with his closed system came at the Apple Worldwide Developer's Conference in June, 2011. This was when Steve introduced a new service Apple had developed for its users. It was called 'iCloud'.

Getting all of Apple's new products to run smoothly with each other was, in Steve's words, "driving us crazy".

'MobileMe', the $99-a-year service Apple had introduced in June, 2008, had developed so many problems that Apple had decided to abandon it. This was because the computer had to act as the hub for all the information users needed to connect with on their various devices. Apple were replacing MobileMe with iCloud, which would be free. The 'cloud' referred to distant servers* which could hold enormous amounts of information. The computer, like all other devices would use iCloud to connect to this information. This would solve the difficult problems of making different devices work smoothly together. Steve gave an example. "From now on," he said, "Apple will have more than eighteen million songs available on its iCloud servers."

This time Steve could only give the audience his words. There was no wonderful new product to hold in his hands. There was nothing to take the audience's attention away from one very sad and troubling fact:

Steve looked and sounded terribly ill.

C H A P T E R   1 1

The Final Battle

"I've had a very lucky career, a very lucky life. I've done all that I can do." (Steve Jobs)

By 2010, Apple had risen from failure to become the most successful company in the world. That was amazing enough. What was even more amazing was the fact that Steve had achieved this while fighting a life or death battle with cancer.

As with most things, Steve had a habit of ignoring what was real. Others referred to this as 'magical thinking'. It was a fault as well as a strength. On the positive side, it allowed him to focus on the perfection of what he wanted to achieve. It also encouraged everyone around him and led to the creation of wonderful products. On the negative side, it allowed him to ignore serious issues that needed to be dealt with. Nowhere was this more true than in relation to his health. Several times over the years, Steve had mentioned to both friends and family his belief that he would not live a long life. This idea that he may be running out of time made him impatient with anything that got in the way of his goals. In the case of his health, he ignored the problem for so long that by the time he decided to act, the situation had grown much worse.

These problems started some time in 1997, when Steve was trying to run both Pixar and Apple. He was in the habit of working sixteen hours a day or more, and coming home so tired he could hardly speak. During this time, he developed stones in his kidneys*. Eventually the pain got so bad that he went to the doctor. The doctor told him what the problem was and said that the stones would have to be removed. Steve had the operation and everything seemed fine. But then, in October, 2003, five years after the operation, he happened to meet the doctor who had treated him. She advised him to get a medical examination, just to check that his kidneys were still OK. The examination would be neither long nor difficult, so Steve agreed.

The results of the examination showed that Steve's kidneys were fine but that there appeared to be a small shadow on his pancreas*. Further tests needed to be done, the doctor told him. This time, Steve didn't follow her advice. But she kept reminding him how important it was to have the tests done. Laurene agreed. Steve finally made an appointment and had them done the following week.

The news was not good. The shadow turned out to be cancer. Luckily, it was a form of cancer that could be removed if they acted quickly. But Steve was against the idea of surgery*. Instead, he preferred to explore what he called more 'natural' treatments. These included strict vegetarian* diets, 'natural' medicines, and other alternative treatments.

None of these worked, and as time went on friends, family, and colleagues pressed him to have the surgery done. Even his natural health doctor advised him to have the operation.

Steve finally agreed and the operation was done in Stanford University Medical Centre on July 31st, 2004.

Part of Steve's pancreas was removed, but tests done after the operation showed that the cancer had spread to other parts of his body. It seemed clear that if Steve had acted nine months earlier, this may not have happened.

As always, Steve ignored the seriousness of the situation. He told his colleagues at Apple that everything was OK and that he would soon be back at work. Deep inside, he probably realised he was fighting the battle of his life. He just didn't want the rest of the world to know about it.

However, the knowledge that the earlier feelings he had expressed about dying relatively young might well come true, led him to give the most remarkable speech of his career.

It took place at Stanford University in June, 2005.

Steve had been asked to address all the students who had successfully completed their studies and were moving on to a variety of professional careers. In the third part of his speech, Steve talked about death.

"Remembering that I'll be dead soon has been an important tool in helping me make the big choices in life," he told his young audience. "Everything: pride, embarrassment, failure. All these things disappear in the face of death. They leave only what is truly important. And that is, to follow your heart."

• • •

For almost three years following that speech, Steve's health didn't appear to become any worse. But then, by early 2008, he was in pain, looked extremely thin, and had almost completely lost his appetite. His doctors told him that the cancer had spread to his liver*. The only hope was for Steve to have a liver transplant*.

At first, Steve said no, but by January, 2009, he had been persuaded to have the operation. First, they had to find a donor*. In the meantime, all Steve and his family could do was wait.

As he was waiting for the operation, Steve was aware of the increasing number of stories about his health appearing in the news. Apple was not saying whether the stories were true or not. This made people believe that they were true and it was having a bad effect on the value of the company. For a lot of people, Apple's success was due to one man: Steve Jobs. Without him, they feared the company would fall, as it had before. Steve decided to act before the situation became any worse. In February, 2009, he released a statement saying that his health problems were not serious and he would soon be well again. This was untrue, but it stopped the value of Apple going down any further.

On March 21st, 2009, a liver became available and Steve was rushed to hospital for the operation. His family were a great support during this time. By now, he and Laurene had two children: a boy named Reed, born in 1991, and a girl called Eve, born in 1998. Steve's daughter by Chrisann, Lisa, had also been living with the family. Of all the children, Steve was closest to Reed. Above all, he wanted to live long enough to see his son finish college. His relationship with his daughters was not so easy. Eve was very independent and Lisa often got angry with her father and blamed him for the way he had treated her and Chrisann in the past. However, their relationship improved during Steve's illness.

The doctors reported that Steve's surgery had been a success. This was not entirely true. There were signs that the cancer may have spread beyond the liver but the doctors hoped to control this with the use of special drugs. For now, Steve, his family, and Apple were delighted.

For the next two months, he gradually recovered his strength and by the end of May was back at the company he loved.

His old colleagues expected him to be quieter, with less energy and less aggression.

They were wrong. On his first day back, Steve criticised the engineers, threw away some marketing plans he didn't agree with and attacked many of the things the company had been doing while he'd been away.

At the end of the day, he said, "I had the greatest time being back today."

This shows that Steve's aggression was not intended to hurt people. It was simply a way of expressing his views and getting others to work hard to achieve them. This is certainly what both Tim Cook and Jony Ive understood and they were not at all worried by Steve's behaviour.

Throughout most of 2010, while Steve was working on the iPad 2, he was as focused and enthusiastic as ever. Stories about his health were taken less seriously and the company's value had never been higher. Sadly, the situation did not last.

In early November, Steve began to feel more pain throughout his body. He was also losing his appetite. By Christmas, he had lost so much weight that he was the thinnest he had ever been. The cancer was back and Steve was forced to leave work for treatment.

His doctors fought the cancer with a variety of special drugs. Some of these worked for a while but it soon became clear that they were fighting a losing battle. Pictures of Steve looking thin and ill began to appear on the internet. Despite this, he did his best to keep going. When he felt strong enough he would occasionally return to the company for a few days, or appear at special events. His launch of the iPad 2 in San Francisco on March 3rd, 2011, immediately sent the value of Apple shares up even though he looked extremely sick.

During this period, many people came to visit him at his home. One of these was the former US President, Bill Clinton. But perhaps the most interesting was from Bill Gates. The respect they had for each other was clear during this visit. They talked like old friends for over three hours. The visit ended with them shaking hands and praising each other.

Two months after Bill Gates' visit, Steve's doctors discovered that the cancer had spread to his bones. He was in pain, finding it difficult to either eat or sleep and knew that he no longer had the energy to continue as CEO of Apple. He would have to give up his job.

He decided to do this in person. At eleven o'clock on the morning of August 24th, 2011, Steve arrived at Apple's head office in a wheelchair*. He had with him a letter explaining his decision to no longer continue as Apple's CEO. He was taken to the boardroom. Following the usual custom, all the board members with positions inside the company, left the room. Only the outside board members, all close friends of Steve's remained. These now included the former US vice-president, Al Gore.

Steve left his wheelchair and began to read his letter out loud. It was short, clear but full of emotion:

"I have always said," he began, "that if a day ever came when I was unable to do my job, that I would be the first to let you know. Unfortunately, that day has come. I believe Apple's brightest days are ahead of it and I look forward to watching and helping its success in a new role."

There were tears in the eyes of the board members as Steve folded the letter and handed it to Al Gore. Al was the first to speak and he did so by saying that what Steve had achieved at Apple was, "the most incredible thing I've seen in business."

One by one, the board members stood up, walked over to Steve, put their arms around him and left feeling too emotional to say another word.

• • •

At shortly after three o'clock on the afternoon of October 5th, 2011, Steve died at his home in Palo Alto. His wife and children were by his side. The last thing he expressed before he died was the amazing love he felt for his family, with the simple words: "Oh, wow."

Steve's Footprint

The mark Steve left on the world is like a footprint formed in rock. Like the passing of some ancient creature, the signs will never disappear. They are all around us, part of our daily lives, affecting all aspects of our ability to communicate with each other and the world in general. The beauty and excellence of the products he helped create have set the standard in an industry where now only the very best is expected.

To have achieved so much, was it necessary for Steve to show the unpleasant side of his character as much as he did? The answer is probably no. But his rudeness and aggression were often misunderstood. His intention not to hurt people but to get them to produce their best work. With some, he failed. With others, he succeeded. Those like Tim Cook and Jony Ive – who realised that Steve's switches from praise to aggression were the only way he could express himself – were able to focus on work without being bothered by his negative comments. They realised that Steve was, above all, a man of extremes. Things were either 'wonderful' or 'useless'. There was no middle way. Fortunately for Apple and the rest of the world, the 'wonderful' is what he left us.

GLOSSARY

adopted: to legally bring a child who is not yours permanently into your family.

animated: full of enthusiasm

award: a prize or certificate given for doing something really well.

Buddhism: a belief system which says that the best way to end personal suffering is by overcoming your desires.

calligraphy: the art of producing beautiful handwriting.

click: the action of pressing a finger on a computer mouse to perform a function.

cube: an object with six square surfaces which are all the same size.

device: an object, usually mechanical or electronic, that has been made for a particular purpose.

donor: someone who agrees to give their body for medical use after they are dead.

fan: an electrical device which moves air around to create a cool environment.

grade: in the North American school system, the name given to a class where the students are of a similar age or educational ability.

hammer: a heavy piece of metal at the end of a handle which is used as a tool for hitting things.

kidney: the part of your body which produces waste matter, called 'urine', from your blood.

liver: the part of your body that cleans unwanted substances from your blood.

mechanic: a person who repairs or looks after machines.

obsession: something you cannot stop thinking about because you believe it is very important to you.

pancreas: the part of your body that produces substances to help in the digestion of food.

partnership: when two people, organisations, or countries work together.

pregnant: if a female woman or animal is pregnant, they have a baby developing inside their body.

project: an idea or plan you intend to work on and make successful in the future.

rational: the ability to base decisions on reason rather than emotion.

rebel: someone who has rejected many of the values of their family or society.

stylus: a small pointed instrument.

surgery: a medical operation where the body is cut open so that a doctor can repair it.

transplant: to replace a damaged part of a person's body by the same, undamaged, part of another person's body.

Technical words and expressions:

applications (apps) a program or a piece of software designed to fulfil a particular purpose

digital information represented as digits (or numbers), relating to computer technology

download copy (data) from one computer to another or to a disk

Graphic User Interface (GUI) a type of user interface that allows users to interact with electronic devices with images (e.g. icons) rather than text commands

hardware the physical components of a computer system

hub the centre of a network

icon a symbol or graphic representation on screen of a program, option or window

integrated circuit an electronic circuit on a small piece of silicon which performs the same function as a larger circuit of discrete components

laptop a portable personal computer

microprocessor a very small silicone chip

mouse a rollerball in a small handheld case which, when rolled on a flat surface, moves the cursor on a computer screen

online something which is delivered via, or can be viewed on, the internet is said to be online

operating system the low level software that supports a computer's basic functions

silicon chip a small piece of silicon which conducts electricity

software programs and other operating information used by a computer

tablet a mobile computer integrated into a flat touch screen.

touch screen a screen which reacts to being touched by a human finger or hand

virus a computer program which can replicate itself and spread from one computer to another

website a designated area of the internet where people or companies can upload information

Business words and expressions

board the group of directors who advise and oversee the management of a company

CEO Chief Executive Officer: the most senior person managing a company or organisation

chairman the most senior director on the board

consumer the person who buys or consumes a product or service

corporation a large company or group of companies authorised to act as a single entity and recognised by law

investor someone who gives money to a scheme, shares or property with the expectation of achieving a profit

launch to introduce a new product to the market with an attention-grabbing event or party

logo a graphic image used by commercial companies or organisations to promote instant recognition

market share the proportion of the market supplied by a company's product or service

personnel the people employed by a company, also known as human resources